All Active

35 Inclusive Physical Activities

Kiwi Bielenberg, MEd

Library of Congress Cataloging-in-Publication Data

Bielenberg, Kiwi, 1972-
All active : 35 inclusive physical activities / Kiwi Bielenberg.
  p. cm.
ISBN-13: 978-0-7360-7214-4 (soft cover)
ISBN-10: 0-7360-7214-4 (soft cover)
1. Physical education for children--Study and teaching (Elementary) I. Title.
GV443.B475 2008
372.86--dc22
                2007031767

ISBN-10: 0-7360-7214-4
ISBN-13: 978-0-7360-7214-4

Acquisitions Editors: Scott Wikgren and Bonnie Pettifor Vreeman; **Developmental Editor:** Jacqueline Eaton Blakley; **Assistant Editor:** Jackie Walker; **Copyeditor:** Patrick Connolly; **Proofreader:** Anne Meyer Byler; **Permission Manager:** Carly Breeding; **Graphic Designer:** Nancy Rasmus; **Graphic Artist:** Dawn Sills; **Cover Designer:** Keith Blomberg; **Photographer (cover):** Artistic Photography; **Photographer (interior):** Artistic Photography; photo on page 11 by Valerie Scofield; **Visual Production Assistant:** Joyce Brumfield; **Photo Office Assistant:** Jason Allen; **Art Manager:** Kelly Hendren; **Associate Art Manager:** Alan L. Wilborn; **Illustrator:** Accurate Art; **Printer:** Victor Graphics

We thank Northfield Public Schools in Northfield, MN, for assistance in providing the location for the photo shoot for this book.

Printed in the United States of America   10   9   8   7   6   5   4   3   2   1

Human Kinetics
Web site: www.HumanKinetics.com

United States: Human Kinetics
P.O. Box 5076
Champaign, IL 61825-5076
800-747-4457
e-mail: humank@hkusa.com

Canada: Human Kinetics
475 Devonshire Road Unit 100
Windsor, ON N8Y 2L5
800-465-7301 (in Canada only)
e-mail: orders@hkcanada.com

Europe: Human Kinetics
107 Bradford Road
Stanningley
Leeds LS28 6AT, United Kingdom
+44 (0) 113 255 5665
e-mail: hk@hkeurope.com

Australia: Human Kinetics
57A Price Avenue
Lower Mitcham, South Australia 5062
08 8372 0999
e-mail: info@hkaustralia.com

New Zealand: Human Kinetics
Division of Sports Distributors NZ Ltd.
P.O. Box 300 226 Albany
North Shore City
Auckland
0064 9 448 1207
e-mail: info@humankinetics.co.nz

Don't let what you
cannot do interfere
with what you can do.

—John Wooden

To my past, present, and future Northfield students, your love for movement in its purest form has encouraged me to write down these ideas that have gone from my brain to your muscles.

To Aleisha, Ryan, and Rachel, thanks for always teaching me about taking time to play. I love you.

And to God, the giver of every great idea.

Contents

Activity Finder   viii
Preface   xi

1 Fitness and Movement Activities   1

2 Object Manipulation Activities   33

3 Balance and Coordination Activities   51

4 Combination Activities   65

About the Author   81

Activity Finder

This simple table will help you locate activities that are best suited for any particular context you encounter. It lists the activities in alphabetical order and shows you at a glance each activity's estimated setup time, ideal location, cardiovascular activity level, emphasized skills, and page number.

Setup time

Less than 15 minutes

15 to 30 minutes

More than 30 minutes

Location

Indoors **I**

Outdoors **O**

Both **B**

Activity level

Low

Medium

High

Activity name	Setup time	Indoors or outdoors	Activity level	Skills	Page
Balance Beam Basketball	⏰⏰	I	♡♡	Balance and coordination	56
Ball Pit Bulldozer	⏰	I	♡♡♡	Combination activities	66
Basketball ABCs	⏰⏰	I	♡♡	Object manipulation	48
Bolster Bowling	⏰	I	♡♡	Object manipulation	44
Case of the Missing Spiders	⏰⏰	I	♡♡	Combination Activities	72
Clothespin Fitness	⏰⏰	B	♡♡♡	Fitness and movement	22
Comic Book Clash	⏰⏰⏰	I	♡♡	Object manipulation	42
Don't Drop Your Ice Cream	⏰	B	♡♡	Balance and coordination	60
Dot-to-Dot	⏰⏰	I	♡♡	Balance and coordination	62
Fish for Your Name	⏰⏰⏰	I	♡	Balance and coordination	52
Gift Bag Scramble	⏰⏰	I	♡♡	Fitness and movement	26
Magnificent Lights Maze	⏰⏰⏰	I	♡♡	Fitness and movement	14
Mat Boat Rescue	⏰	I	♡♡	Fitness and movement	20
Monster Truck Knockdown	⏰⏰	B	♡♡	Combination activities	74
Oh, That's Hot!	⏰	B	♡♡	Fitness and movement	8
Pick a Piece of Pumpkin	⏰⏰⏰	I	♡♡	Object manipulation	40
Pick a Stick	⏰⏰	B	♡♡♡	Fitness and movement	12
Piece It Together	⏰⏰	I	♡♡	Fitness and movement	4

(continued)

(continued)

Activity name	Setup time	Indoors or outdoors	Activity level	Skills	Page
Pop That Bubble!	🕐	I	♡♡	Object manipulation	38
Rainbow Hoop Shoot	🕐🕐	B	♡♡	Object manipulation	36
Rainbow Snow Tower	🕐	O	♡♡	Combination activities	70
Ready, Set, Pull!	🕐	I	♡♡	Combination activities	68
Roll the Dice, Grab the Mice	🕐	B	♡♡♡	Fitness and movement	16
Rollin' for Wristbands	🕐	I	♡♡♡	Fitness and movement	2
Ropes and Towers	🕐🕐	I	♡♡	Combination activities	77
Safari	🕐	B	♡♡	Fitness and movement	24
Shake, Balance, and Go!	🕐🕐🕐	B	♡♡	Balance and coordination	58
Snowmen Versus Elves	🕐🕐	B	♡♡	Object manipulation	34
Sticker Hunt	🕐🕐	I	♡♡♡	Fitness and movement	18
Treasure Map	🕐🕐🕐	B	♡♡♡	Fitness and movement	6
Trim That Tree!	🕐🕐🕐	I	♡♡	Object manipulation	46
Turkey Feather Bingo	🕐🕐🕐	I	♡♡	Fitness and movement	30
Watch Your Step	🕐🕐	I	♡	Balance and coordination	54
We're Hungry	🕐	I	♡♡♡	Fitness and movement	28
X Marks The Snow	🕐🕐	O	♡	Fitness and movement	10

Preface

After 10 years of teaching physical education, I have come to grips with one simple truth: *Students love to move when there is a purpose and goal.* I've learned that students of all abilities seem to be motivated by three common goals:

1. Searching for hidden items
2. Collecting objects
3. Completing a task that changes the appearance of something

This book is a collection of activities that use these three elements to give students the motivation to move. But more than just a book of games, *All Active* is a *framework,* showing you how to use equipment in game situations that are motivating for students.

As physical educators, we use equipment to achieve specific results. For example, we use scooters to work on balance and lower-body strength. We also use exercise balls, balance beams, stretch bands, minitrampolines, and students' own locomotor movements to work toward specific goals. The activities in this book show you innovative, flexible ways to use equipment and movement to support your goals for your students. In other words, there is a purpose behind their practice.

The book's activities are designed to be customizable and transferable. For example, if an activity lists a scooter as the means to go from point A to point B, you may replace the scooter with another mode of travel: moving on a bouncy ball, crab walking, skipping, pulling a partner on a blanket, and so on. As a teacher, you are called to create the most meaningful and purposeful setting to meet the individual needs of your students. These activities allow you the freedom to do so.

The 35 activities in *All Active* were created with elementary students in mind. All the skills and challenges are developmentally appropriate for kids in kindergarten through fifth grade. Because these are framework ideas, you may choose specific skills to be used within the activity based on the ages of your students. For example, kindergarteners may be asked to strike a balloon in the air with a foam paddle down to a line and back. However, for fifth graders, you may choose to extend the activity, asking them to bounce a tennis ball on alternating faces of a racket down to a line and back. You can also alter distance to make the activity more developmentally appropriate. Moving a starting cone closer to or farther away from their goal can greatly change the difficulty of an activity.

Many of the game ideas in this book are geared toward smaller groups of students (4 to 8 children). If you teach in an adapted physical education setting, these activities will most likely work as written. However, if you teach regular physical education—with groups of 25 or more students—the following suggestions may help you provide students with the most activity time possible. (And of course, you need to be creative and do everything you can to avoid having large groups of students standing in line and being inactive.)

- **Use the activity as one of several stations you have set up for the day.** If you are teaching a lesson on basketball dribbling, for example, there may be several stations you set up to practice that skill. One station might involve dribbling around cones, another would involve dribbling around a defender, and a third station could be the activity Pick a Piece of Pumpkin. By creating stations for a physical education class of 30 students, you can drastically decrease the wait time—only 10 students would be at each station (5 students on each team for Pick a Piece of Pumpkin).

- **Add more teams and more equipment to the activity.** In the game Gift Bag Scramble, the instructions say to place 2 starting cones and divide students into 2 teams. However, if you have a class of 30 students, 15 students in each line would mean a huge wait time and much inactivity. Instead of placing only 2 cones, you can put out 10 cones in a line, with a team of 3 people behind each cone. When there are more students, you will also need more types of equipment that the students can use for transportation in this game. Instead of only providing one scooter and one bouncy ball, get creative about other equipment that students could move on. For example, you could put out three scooters, three bungee jumpers, two bouncy balls, and two pairs of foam stilts. That way, enough equipment is available to accommodate all 10 teams.

By simply thinking through these ideas of using station work, increasing the number of teams, and increasing the amount of equipment, you will see that the activities can easily be modified to work with larger classes.

All Active is divided into four chapters, each with its own specific motor focus. Browse chapter 1, Fitness and Movement Activities, when you are looking for ideas to get your students active. The games in chapter 1 offer a variety of cardiorespiratory activities that also involve practice of locomotor movement (e.g., skipping, galloping, hopping). Chapter 2, Object Manipulation Activities, offers creative ideas for practicing skills that involve object control, such as throwing, kicking, striking, shooting, and dribbling a ball. In chapter 3, Balance and Coordination Activities, you'll find activities that enable students to work on the skills of static balance, body control, and body awareness. This chapter also includes activities that involve using eye–hand coordination to balance and control a given object, such as balancing a ball on the end of a paper towel tube. Chapter 4, Combination Activities, contains games that are twofold in their purpose. The first part of an activity might consist of a challenge involving locomotor movement, and the second part of the activity might require executing a skill with a ball. These combination activities involve multiple objectives in more than one skill area.

For each activity, the following sections are presented to help you set up the activity and successfully instruct your students:

- **Objective** explains the purpose of the activity and what the goal is for students.

- **Equipment** lists the types and number of equipment items needed for that activity.

- **Setup** gives you directions to prepare the activity before students arrive. Clear explanations about the preparation and placement of equipment are provided in this section.

- **Instructions** offers a step-by-step explanation of how to carry out the given activity. Details of your role are given, along with clear guidelines for determining when the activity is complete.

- **Teacher Tips** gives you ideas for various ways to use equipment or adjust the activity in order to provide a different level of challenge. Because these are "framework" activities, this section offers additional ideas for how students can move or participate in the activity. This section may also describe ways to adapt the activity for students in wheelchairs or students using walkers.

It is my hope that this book of ideas will add to the great job of teaching you are already doing and that you and your students will find more purpose in movement. Have fun!

Fitness and Movement Activities

Rollin' for Wristbands

OBJECTIVE

Students collect six different colors of wristbands as they scooter around the gym.

EQUIPMENT

- ✯ Scooters
- ✯ Cones
- ✯ Colored wristbands (six different colors per student)

SETUP

Spread out cones throughout the gym (enough for six cones per student). Under each cone, hide one wristband.

INSTRUCTIONS

1. Tell students to collect a full rainbow of wristbands and to put them on their arms as they find each one.
2. All students move at the same time, and they each try to collect their wristbands independently. If students peek under a cone and see a color of wristband they are already wearing, they need to cover the wristband back up and move to another cone. If students find a cone that is empty—that is, someone has already taken the wristband from under that cone—they need to move to another cone.
3. The activity ends when all students have all six colors (red, blue, green, yellow, orange, purple) of wristbands on their arms.

TEACHER TIPS

- ✯ For students using a walker or those who have other limitations in leg strength, use lightweight cones that can be kicked over easily.
- ✯ Allow students in wheelchairs to knock the cones over with hockey sticks.
- ✯ Instead of using scooters, allow students to bike, run, skip, and so forth to each cone.
- ✯ Shorten the activity by tipping over the empty cones so that students don't need to check those.
- ✯ For a greater challenge, have students change scooter position or change their mode of movement each time they find one of their wristbands.

Piece It Together

OBJECTIVE

Students collect pieces of a large jigsaw puzzle by completing exercises in a fitness circuit. With those pieces, they work cooperatively to complete the puzzle.

EQUIPMENT

- Large colorful floor puzzle (appropriate developmental level)
- Cones (six to eight)
- Fitness station equipment (exercise ball, stretch band, bungee jumper, minitrampoline, beanbags and bucket, scooters)

SETUP

Create six to eight fitness stations spread out in different areas of the gym. Place a cone with a picture sign by each station. Here are some examples of the stations I use:

- Students perform 25 seated bounces on an exercise ball.
- Students perform 15 stretch-band pulls overhead.
- Students hop on a bungee jumper down and around a cone.
- Students perform 20 jumps on a minitrampoline.
- Students perform a shuttle run. Three beanbags are placed on the starting line. Students run fast with one beanbag down to a bucket, drop the beanbag into the bucket, and then run back to retrieve the second beanbag, and so on.
- Students scooter on their bellies down and around a cone.
- Students perform 10 scooter burpees. With their hands flat on the ground and their toes resting on a scooter, the students move their legs slowly in and out, holding the wheelbarrow stance with their arms.

Dump out the puzzle pieces in the middle of the gym so that the pieces are all mixed up.

INSTRUCTIONS

1. Have each student begin at a different fitness station. It is ideal to have only one student at each station to avoid waiting time. However, if there are more students than the number of stations, you can simply add equipment to allow more students to be active at each station. Give a signal to rotate after approximately two to three minutes, depending on the skill level of students and how long it takes them to complete a fitness activity.

2. Once they have completed the activity for their station, students choose a puzzle piece from the big mixed-up pile and bring it over to the designated area where the puzzle will be put together. For the fitness circuit time, students should simply collect the pieces and drop them off at the puzzle area.

3. At the end of the class time (I usually have each student move through all the stations two or three times to allow for many puzzle pieces to be collected), students spend the last five minutes putting the whole puzzle together as a group.

TEACHER TIPS

☆ To help students with the puzzle, put together the puzzle's border before the activity begins. Place the completed border at the drop-off area, then place the middle puzzle pieces at each station. This will save time and allow students to complete the puzzle faster.

☆ If you don't have enough equipment for students at each station, have students find a partner to work with. One partner stays at the puzzle area and works on putting together the puzzle while the other partner completes the given fitness station task. Partners then change positions when you give a signal to switch.

☆ If the puzzle has many pieces, or if you are using this for a shorter activity, allow students to carry three to five puzzle pieces to the drop-off area after completing a fitness station.

Treasure Map

OBJECTIVE

Students follow their treasure map to find the six hidden colors (crayons or markers) in the proper order.

EQUIPMENT

- Six cones
- Six crayons or drawing markers of different colors
- Individual treasure maps for each student

SETUP

Note: Ideally, this activity is done outside in a large area.

Before class, print a variety of treasure maps for the students. Put each student's name at the top of each map to personalize it. I also add clip art of various solid-colored objects to provide a visual aid that helps students identify which color they are trying to find next.

To set up, place the six cones so that they are spread out 50 to 100 feet (15 to 30 meters) from each other. When placing the cones, put them in interesting places (e.g., on the playground slide, behind the backstop, and so on) while also making sure the cones are visible. Under each cone, place one drawing marker or crayon. The colors of the markers or crayons must match the colored items on the treasure maps you hand out.

INSTRUCTIONS

1. Hand out the individual treasure maps to students.
2. Explain that the students need to try to find all six colors, but they must do it in the order their map tells them. This activity provides a cardiorespiratory workout, so you should encourage students to pace themselves. As an example, look at the sample treasure map on page 7. If Julie's first color is yellow, she must run and check the various cones until she finds the yellow crayon under a cone. If she comes to a cone with the incorrect color, she may not mark her map; instead, she must hide the crayon back under the cone and continue the hunt for the yellow crayon.
3. Once students find the correct color, they should use that crayon to circle the corresponding number on their map, thus proving that they found the crayon (e.g., when Julie finds the yellow crayon, she would use it to circle the number 1 by the word *yellow* on her map). After circling the number of a color that has been found, students then move on to hunt for their next color (e.g., after circling the number 1, Julie would move on to hunt for the red crayon).

4. The activity ends when all students have marked all six colors shown on their maps and have returned to the instructor to hand in their completed treasure maps.

TEACHER TIPS

- ⭐ If a large outdoor space isn't available, you may use this activity indoors by having students use various locomotor movements or even scooters.

- ⭐ To increase the distance that students must move, have the students run back to you to show proof of each color as they find it. This also allows you to check the students' understanding of which color they are looking for next.

- ⭐ If the activity is dragging on, with some students forgetting where certain colors are, encourage students who have finished to team up and help their classmates remember where colors are hidden.

Julie's Map	**Henry's Map**

Julie's Map	Henry's Map
1. Yellow ⭐	1. Purple 🦋
2. Red ♥	2. Green 🌲
3. Blue 🎀	3. Orange 🥕
4. Green 🌲	4. Blue 🎀
5. Purple 🦋	5. Red ♥
6. Orange 🥕	6. Yellow ⭐

Oh, That's Hot!

OBJECTIVE

Students complete fitness activities through a variation of the game Hot Potato.

EQUIPMENT

- Foam football
- Recipe card strips
- Music
- Poly spot floor markers

SETUP

Do you have an old foam football lying around, or maybe a foam ball with a chunk taken out of it? Use it for this game! Cut a small slit in the foam ball that you will use. The slit should be deep enough to hold a folded strip of paper. On strips of paper or recipe cards (the sturdier paper is easier to push into the ball), write out as many fitness activities as there are students in your class. Each strip will have only one activity written on it. Here are some examples:

- Run and touch five red things in the gym.
- Do 10 mountain climbers.
- Moving like your favorite animal, travel to the door and back.
- Crab walk to the middle circle.

Keep these fitness strips next to you during the activity; you will be folding one for each new turn and pushing it into the slit of the ball. Use the poly spot floor markers to create a circle. The circle should be small enough so that each student will be able to reach his neighbor.

INSTRUCTIONS

1. Tell students to sit in a circle, with each student sitting on one of the poly spot markers.
2. Push the first slip of paper inside the foam ball (make sure you leave a little corner sticking out to grab).
3. Start the music.
4. Students quickly pass the "hot ball" clockwise around the circle until the music stops. The person who is holding the ball when the music stops gets to pull out the paper and read what it says. Everyone participates in the fitness activity listed. Once the activity has been completed by everyone, students find their same poly spot, sit down, and get ready for another round.

5. Push the next fitness strip inside the ball, begin the music, and repeat the same sequence.

6. The activity ends when all students have had a turn to pull out and read one of the fitness strips. (You should intentionally stop the music on each student in the class.)

TEACHER TIPS

✪ Instead of using a foam ball, have students pass around plastic Easter eggs with the fitness activity strips folded up inside. When the music stops, students open up the plastic egg and take out the piece of paper.

✪ Enlarge the circle of students and have them toss the ball across the circle. Instead of simply handing the ball to the person on their left, students call out someone's name across the circle and throw the hot football to that person.

✪ If possible, you should have an educational assistant help with the music and keep track of which students have already had a turn. This will free you up to load the new fitness activity strip and to observe or help students performing the given fitness challenge.

✪ If you have students who are unable to make lateral movements to hand off the ball, you may allow them to use a wheelchair ramp to roll the ball down and across the circle to another student.

X Marks the Snow

OBJECTIVE

Students hunt for Xs in the snow and dig to find buried Easter eggs. Everyone loves a fun Easter egg hunt—but in the snow? This is a great activity for a snowy winter day when you can't stand being inside any longer. It can be done as a race or just a fun activity to enjoy the outdoors during the winter.

EQUIPMENT

- Colorful plastic Easter eggs
- Spray bottle
- Food coloring
- Water

SETUP

Bury plastic Easter eggs in the snow. The number you hide will depend on how large an area you have to work with and how many students you have. For a class of six students, I usually bury about 30 eggs, spreading them out 15 to 20 feet (4.5 to 6.1 meters) from each other; each student tries to find and dig up 5 eggs. Fill a spray bottle with water and food coloring, and then spray a colored X on the snow over each general area where an egg is buried.

INSTRUCTIONS

1. Tell students they are going for an egg hunt in the snow!
2. On your signal, students hunt for the Xs in the snow and dig with their hands until they find an egg.
3. The activity ends when all students have found all their eggs.

TEACHER TIPS

- Use sleds and have students work together in partners. One student pulls the other to the first X, the partners dig for the egg, and then they switch riders.
- To make it extra fun, assign each student her own color for where she will dig. Use different colored water when spraying on the Xs. One student looks for the green Xs, another student digs in areas with a blue X, and so on.
- Try the same activity with students wearing snowshoes!

☆ If students are searching for more eggs than they can hold, give each student a basket or bucket to collect the eggs in.

☆ If snow is not available, this is a fun activity to use in a sandbox. Bury the eggs under the sand, and use markers on top of the sand—such as little flags or rubber animals—that give students clues for where to dig.

Pick a Stick

OBJECTIVE

Students run warm-up laps to collect Popsicle sticks, and they hunt for a yarn ball that matches each stick.

EQUIPMENT

- Popsicle sticks
- Jar to hold the sticks
- Small, solid-colored yarn balls
- Coloring markers or crayons
- Plastic stacking cups
- Bucket

SETUP

Color the ends of wooden Popsicle sticks with crayons or markers to match the colors of yarn balls you have. Decide how many warm-up laps you would like your students to run. Multiply that number by how many students are in the class to determine how many Popsicle sticks you will need. For example, if the students are going to run three laps, and you have four students in the class, then you'll need a total of 12 Popsicle sticks. Place these colored sticks in a jar near the door where students enter the gym. In the middle of the gym, spread out 12 plastic stacking cups. Under each cup, hide one yarn ball (the colors of the yarn balls should correspond to the colored sticks).

INSTRUCTIONS

1. Students run one full lap around the playing area, beginning in the spot where they enter the gym for class.
2. When students get back to the starting spot, they each choose a Popsicle stick and check its color.
3. Students run to the middle of the gym to search under cups for the matching color of yarn ball.
4. Once they find their match, students bring the Popsicle stick and matching ball over to show you. Students then drop the items in a "put-away bucket" and begin their second lap.
5. After completing the second lap, students pick another stick, search for the matching ball, and so on.

6. The activity ends when all students have completed their warm-up laps and have found all the matches to their Popsicle sticks.

TEACHER TIPS

⭐ Be creative about what else you could hide. Some other ideas include the following:

  ⭐ Small plastic animals under cups

  ⭐ Fun-shaped beanbags under dome cones

  ⭐ Plastic Easter eggs under cones

  ⭐ Colored shapes, letters, or numbers (cut out of colored paper) under Frisbees

⭐ To increase the challenge, have students switch locomotor skills each lap (e.g., lap 1 = run, lap 2 = slide sideways, lap 3 = move like your favorite animal).

Magnificent Lights Maze

OBJECTIVE

Students maneuver through a lighted maze, performing a variety of tasks.

EQUIPMENT

- Electric Christmas lights
- Tables
- Tape
- Scooters

SETUP

For a change of scenery, surprise your students with a cool maze of lights in a different room than you're normally in. Check to see if any rooms in your school are not used during your physical education time. If possible, find a room with tables or desks already in it. Be sure to check with your school custodian about safety precautions for your strings of lights.

To set up, create a maze with desks and tables. The maze should include various turns and changes of direction. String the Christmas lights in a pathway along the floor, and hang them from the tables (icicle lights work well) to create walls of light for the maze. You can also use foam swim noodles to create a bridge between two tables or two large cones. Attach lights across this bridge that students duck under. To make a tunnel for students to scooter under, simply lay folded mats across two tables. This activity takes a good amount of time to set up, so plan ahead. It is worth your effort to see the students' excitement when they are going through the maze. For the full effect, make sure all the room's lights are off.

INSTRUCTIONS

1. The first student in line sits or lies on a scooter and maneuvers through the lighted maze.
2. When the first student gets halfway through the maze, the next student in line begins his turn.
3. The activity ends when each student has had a specified number of turns completing the maze.

TEACHER TIPS

- Be creative about how to have students move through the maze. Other ideas for their movement include using the crab walk, bear walk, or seal walk; slithering like a snake; and moving on tiptoe.

✫ Students who use wheelchairs or walkers may lie on their backs on a full-body scooter (use a large Velcro strap for safety). An adult or another student may pull them through the maze. These students will love the lights, especially when they are pulled under the lighted bridge.

✫ For a greater challenge, add an additional task for students to do as they move through the maze. For example, have them sit on a scooter while pushing a ball through the maze with a miniature hockey stick.

✫ For added effects, use Christmas lawn decorations as obstacles or as things that students are trying to collect while they go through the maze (e.g., large candy cane decorations, plastic elves). If these decorations (e.g., candy canes) don't have a solid base, cones may be used to hold them in place.

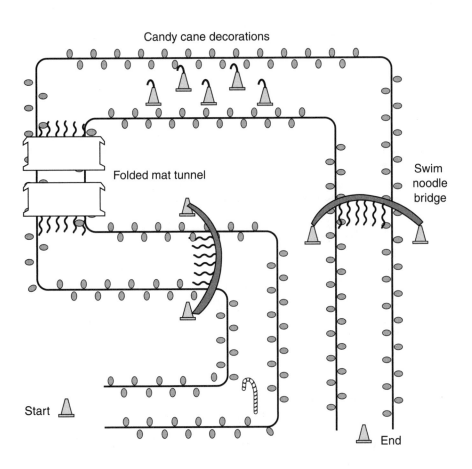

Roll the Dice, Grab the Mice

OBJECTIVE

Students collect mice and distribute them to their correct home (this is a good warm-up activity).

EQUIPMENT

- ✡ One or two large foam dice
- ✡ Small rubber or plastic toy mice (various colors)
- ✡ Buckets or Frisbees that match the colors of mice

SETUP

Spread out all the plastic mice around the floor of the gym. I happen to have a bunch (over 50) of green, blue, and red rubber mice, but you may use any solid-colored animal or object that you'd like (it just may not rhyme as nicely). As a guideline, it would be good to use about 10 mice per student.

INSTRUCTIONS

1. Tell students to meet in the middle circle. This is the dice-rolling area.
2. The first student rolls one or two dice and counts the dots. The teacher then says, "We rolled the dice, now . . . ," and the students say, "Grab the mice!"
3. Everyone runs as fast as they can to pick up mice. Each student picks up the number of mice indicated by the rolled dice.
4. Students run to bring the mice to their matching colored home (located in different corners of the gym). Blue mice get dropped in the blue Frisbee or bucket, red mice find their home in the red Frisbee or bucket, and so forth. Once everyone has helped the mice for that round find their home, the students meet back in the middle circle.
5. The next student rolls the dice, and everyone collects that number of mice.
6. The activity ends once everyone has had a turn to roll the dice or when all the mice have found their home.

TEACHER TIPS

- ✡ Try this game outdoors and spread out the mice over a larger area. In larger spaces, students could work together as a team. Use two foam dice so that the number could get as large as 12 mice to collect (as a team).

To motivate students to go as fast as they can, you or a student may play the role of a cat who will catch the mice if they don't get to their homes. Crawl around on all fours toward the mice on the floor, and play up your disappointment when a student picks up a mouse before the cat could get there.

Sticker Hunt

OBJECTIVE

Students try to fill up their sticker card by scootering around the gym and searching for the matching stickers under cones.

EQUIPMENT

- ✯ Individual sticker cards for each student
- ✯ Sticker sheets that correspond with the cards
- ✯ Scooters (one per student)
- ✯ Dome cones (5 to 10)

SETUP

Decide on the number of stickers you want students to search for (5 to 10). Place that many dome cones around the gym. Under the cones, put a sheet of stickers (these sheets need to contain uniform stickers on the whole sheet). Make an individual sticker card for each student. I use recipe cards for this. Write the student's name at the top of the recipe card, and put the stickers on the card in the order that the student will search for them. Under each sticker, draw a box where the student will stick the matching sticker.

INSTRUCTIONS

1. Hand out the personalized sticker cards to each student.
2. Tell students that this card shows the order in which they need to find their stickers.
3. Each student sits or lies on a scooter and begins scootering around the gym, looking for stickers under different cones.
4. If students check a cone and find a sticker that is not the first one on their card, they need to cover it back up and continue scootering and checking cones until they find their first sticker.
5. When they find a match, they peel off one sticker from the sheet and place it on their card in the first empty spot (e.g., on the second sample card on page 19, the student would place the first sticker in the circle by the heart). Students then continue to search for the second sticker (e.g., the foot), and so on. This is also a memory game, so you should remind students that they need to try to remember where the different stickers are hidden. This will help them when going back to look for stickers that they have previously uncovered.
6. The activity ends when all students have filled their individual sticker cards in the proper order.

TEACHER TIPS

- ⭐ For a greater challenge, put out extra "trick" cones that don't have any stickers under them.

- ⭐ It's a good idea to use different colored cones so that students can associate certain stickers with being under a specific color.

- ⭐ For students using wheelchairs or walkers, use light, upright cones that may be kicked over or knocked over with a bat or hockey stick.

- ⭐ Instead of using scooters, have students bike around the gym to check the cones and collect their stickers.

- ⭐ Use this as a teamwork activity, where partners get one sticker card and take turns pushing their partner on the scooter. When the partners find a sticker, they switch roles, and the other partner sits on the scooter and gets pushed around.

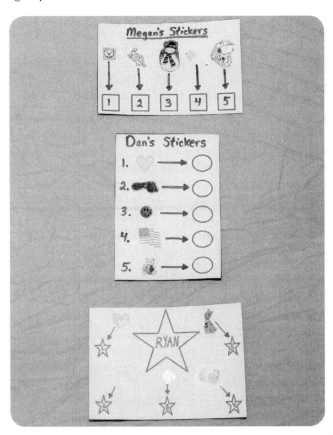

Mat Boat Rescue

OBJECTIVE

Students use their upper- and lower-body strength to push teammates on their mat "boat" to rescue people or animals in trouble.

EQUIPMENT

- ⚝ Folded-up tumbling mats
- ⚝ One opened mat (the "island")
- ⚝ Various baby dolls or stuffed animals

SETUP

Place 10 to 20 baby dolls or stuffed animals around the gym on the floor. Unfold one mat and place it in the center of the gym. This is the island where students may safely stand when getting into their boat.

INSTRUCTIONS

1. Tell students that the gym floor is an ocean, and that there are several people and animals in trouble. The students' mission is to move their boats through the ocean and rescue as many as possible.
2. Divide students into teams of three people. Give each team one folded-up mat boat. All teams move at the same time.
3. Two people sit "pretzel style" on top of the folded-up mat. They are the drivers. The third person is the motor. This person stands behind the boat and pushes it across the ocean. Encourage teams to work together and help the motor determine which direction to push if he can't see a person or animal that needs rescuing.
4. Once they come to a baby doll or animal on the floor, the riders reach down and pull it into their boat.
5. After rescuing a doll or animal, the team goes to the island, gets off the boat, and switches who is riding and who is motoring. The doll or animal just rescued is set on the island to stay.
6. The activity ends when all baby dolls and animals have been rescued from the ocean.

TEACHER TIPS

- ⚝ If students are not strong enough to push a mat with two bodies seated on it, reduce the size of the teams to two people each so that only one rider is on the mat at a time.

✫ To add a challenge, have the boats work together, and time them to see how long it takes to rescue all people and animals from the ocean. Students may want to try again to get a faster time.

Clothespin Fitness

OBJECTIVE

Students complete various cardiorespiratory fitness stations to collect all the colors of clothespins.

EQUIPMENT

- ✄ Clothespins (painted in various colors)
- ✄ Fitness circuit equipment (see ideas in the following section)
- ✄ Cones

SETUP

Decide how many fitness stations you want to set up. These should be activities that take no longer than two minutes to complete. I have painted clothespins in nine colors, so I set up the following nine fitness stations:

- ✄ Students perform 25 seated bounces on an exercise ball.
- ✄ Students perform 50 sideways steps up and down on an aerobics stepper block.
- ✄ Students perform a tire run, stepping with one foot in each "tire," or hula hoop (three turns).
- ✄ Students perform 25 jumps on a bungee jumper.
- ✄ Students crab walk down around a cone and back to the start (three turns).
- ✄ Students perform 25 ski jumps back and forth on two poly spot floor markers.
- ✄ Students push a weighted medicine ball down around a cone and back (three turns).
- ✄ Students scooter down around a cone and back to the start (three turns).
- ✄ Students perform 50 bounces on a minitrampoline.

At each different fitness station, place a cone and the equipment needed for that activity. Attach all the clothespins of one color on one cone (pinch the clothespin and clip it on the top opening of the cone) and create a cone for each color. For example, all the red clothespins go on one station's cone, all the green clothespins go on another station's cone, and so on.

INSTRUCTIONS

1. Tell students they are trying to collect a shirt full of nine clothespins with one of each color.

2. Put one student at each fitness station.

3. Once students have completed an activity, they go to that station's cone, take off a clothespin, and clip it to their shirt.

4. Students then choose a different station that doesn't have anyone at it and move to that station. When they complete that activity, they clip on a clothespin from that station's cone, and so on.

5. The activity ends when every student has collected nine clothespins, having completed all nine fitness station activities.

TEACHER TIPS

✰ If you don't have cones with holes at the top, attach the station clothespins to the edges of poly spot markers.

✰ Sometimes working together with a partner helps increase motivation levels for students. Allow students to move around the stations with a partner; each partner collects her own clothespins.

Safari

OBJECTIVE

Students play a classic memory game by running and finding animal matches under dome cones.

EQUIPMENT

- ✷ Dome cones
- ✷ Small stuffed animals (pairs of the same animal)
- ✷ Hula hoops

SETUP

Place a hula hoop in each corner of the gym. I usually have students play in teams of two; this ensures that there is a lot of activity time for students. For a class of six, you'll need only three hula hoops—each in a different corner. Each hula hoop is the home base for one of the teams.

In the middle of the gym, spread out several dome cones. Hide one animal under each cone, making sure to mix up your matches so they are not right next to each other. The matching pairs don't necessarily need to be the exact same animal, just the same species of animal. So, you hide two frogs, two dogs, two cats, two pigs, and so on. With a class of six students, you may want to use about 24 to 36 cones. This allows all the students to get at least a couple matches. Some students, of course, will have better memories and will find more.

INSTRUCTIONS

1. Divide students into teams of two. Assign each team to a base hula hoop and have them begin there.

2. The first person on each team runs to the middle of the gym and turns over two dome cones. If the animals underneath are a match, students take the animal pair back to their hula hoop and put the animals in their house.

3. If the two animals do not match, students cover them back up with the dome cones, run back to their hula hoop, and tag their teammate.

4. The second teammate runs to the middle of the gym and does the same thing. Encourage the students waiting their turn to watch when the cones are turned over by other teams. This will help them determine where other animals are.

5. The game ends when all the matches have been found and all animals are in a hula hoop home.

TEACHER TIPS

✩ If you can't find enough pairs of stuffed animals, you can always use other objects that match. You can hide small rubber animals or even objects with a certain theme (e.g., things you'd find at a party—hide two party hats, two balloons, two candles). You can use anything that you can find a match for.

✩ Use different-colored cones to hide the animals under. This way, students may use the colors as guides for their teammate ("I think it's under the purple one in the next row over").

✩ For a faster game, pick up the dome cones that matches have been found under. For more of a challenge, leave the empty ones in the game. When playing this way, checking under an empty cone counts as one turn.

Gift Bag Scramble

OBJECTIVE

Students search for gift bags that hold the "special" beanbag with a sticker prize.

EQUIPMENT

- ✵ Assortment of gift bags (10 to 20)
- ✵ Beanbags (one for each gift bag)
- ✵ Scooters
- ✵ Starting cones
- ✵ Bouncy ball (Hoppity Hop)
- ✵ Fun stickers

SETUP

Open up each gift bag and place one regular beanbag inside. In addition, designate "special" gift bags. If you have six students, for example, there should be six bags that contain some type of different special beanbag (e.g., a frog-shaped beanbag). Put a sticker or small prize in each of those special gift bags. Tape the bags shut on top, so no peeking is allowed. Set all the gift bags together near the end line of the gym. Place two cones on the half-court line, 15 feet (4.5 meters) apart from each other. Next to each cone, lay out one scooter and one bouncy ball.

INSTRUCTIONS

1. Divide students evenly into two groups. Each group stands behind one of the cones at the half-court line.

2. The first student in each line chooses either a scooter or a Hoppity Hop ball. Using that equipment, they scooter or bounce down to the end line, where they will find all the gift bags spread out on the floor.

3. Students choose one gift bag, pick it up, and scooter or bounce back to the starting line, tagging the next person in line. Then they check inside their bag to see if they found a special sticker.

4. The next student chooses the scooter or bouncy ball, moves to the gift bags, and so on.

5. The activity ends when all gift bags have been collected. Make sure each student ends up with one special bag with a prize. If a student finds more than one special bag, ask him or her to give the extra bag to a student who did not find a special bag.

TEACHER TIPS

- ✫ Instead of having students scooter or bounce, you can use this as a locomotor activity. Each turn, students choose a different way to move down to the gift bags and back (e.g., moving backward, skipping, or sliding).

- ✫ Students in wheelchairs may wheel themselves and hook the handle of a gift bag using a hockey stick. They could also lie on a long scooter and be pulled by a partner.

- ✫ Instead of putting beanbags inside the gift bags, you can use note cards with letters of the alphabet or numbers written on them. While the next person in line is moving, the remaining students work on lining up letters or numbers in the correct order on the floor.

We're Hungry

OBJECTIVE

Students try to feed the hungry animals by matching play food to the correct animal based on color.

EQUIPMENT

- ✯ Scooters (one per student)
- ✯ Four stuffed animals
- ✯ Play kitchen food
- ✯ Four Frisbees

SETUP

Place a large pile of play kitchen food in the middle of the gym. Put one animal in each corner of the gym, and place an empty Frisbee (turned upside down) in front of each animal—this is the animal's food dish. The color of the Frisbee should match the animal's color. Sort through your play food to make sure there are only items that match the color of the four animals. For example, I have found that the most popular colors of play food are brown (hot dog, chicken), white (egg, ice cream), red (tomato, strawberry), and green (peas, celery). Choose animals that match those food colors (e.g., dog, lamb, lobster, and frog).

INSTRUCTIONS

1. Tell students there are four animals in the gym that are really hungry and need help being fed. However, these are funny animals—they only eat food that is the same color as they are! The dog only wants brown food, the lamb only wants white food, and so forth.

2. Give each student a scooter. All students sit on their scooter in the middle of the gym.

3. On your signal, students choose one piece of food from the pile, figure out which animal would want to eat it (based on color), and scooter over to the animal's food dish to deliver the food.

4. Students drop the food item into the correct animal's dish, scooter back to the middle pile of food, and choose another food item to distribute.

5. The activity ends when all the food is gone and the animals' food dishes are filled.

TEACHER TIPS

- ⭐ Students who use wheelchairs or walkers may carry the chosen food in their lap or in a basket connected to their chair or walker.

- ⭐ Students unable to wheel themselves in a chair may lie on a body scooter and be pulled. They can grab food from the pile, or even use a plastic ball scooper to pick up food items.

Turkey Feather Bingo

OBJECTIVE

Students work together to get a bingo on their team's card by collecting turkey feathers with corresponding numbers.

EQUIPMENT

- Two bingo cards and paper bingo markers (to cover the numbers)
- Starting cones
- Numbered feathers made of construction paper
- Various types of equipment that students can use for "transportation" (e.g., Hoppity Hop ball, scooter, bungee jumper, bike, and so forth)
- Two buckets to collect the paper feathers in

SETUP

Place two starting cones on the midcourt line at least 10 feet (3 meters) apart; the two teams will line up behind these cones. Make two bingo cards—one for each team—as well as bingo markers (paper scraps). Place the bingo cards and markers near each team's starting cone, along with a bucket for collecting used paper feathers.

Cut out turkey feathers from colored construction paper. On the feathers, write the corresponding numbers found on the first team's bingo scorecard. Tape those feathers on the end wall straight ahead of team 1's bingo card. Write team 2's numbers on their feathers and then tape them on the same wall, straight ahead of their starting cone.

In the middle of the gym, place the pieces of equipment that students may use to get down to the feather wall. Choices may include scootering, bouncing on a Hoppity Hop ball, biking, hopping on a bungee jumper, skating on carpet squares, and so forth.

INSTRUCTIONS

1. Divide the students into two teams, and place them behind their team's starting cone.
2. The first student in each line chooses a mode of transportation and moves to the feather wall using that piece of equipment (e.g., bike, scooter).
3. They each pick one feather from their team's wall area and move (i.e., bike, scooter, and so forth) back to their line.
4. The students match the number written on the feather to the corre-

sponding number on their team's bingo card and place a paper marker over that number. Once the corresponding number is covered, students drop the paper feather into their bucket.

5. The next student in each line begins movement once a teammate has found the match on the team's bingo card. Once everyone on a team has had a turn, you should encourage students to choose a different piece of equipment for each new turn.

6. The activity ends when both teams have completed a bingo (five numbers in a row going vertically, horizontally, or diagonally) on their team's card.

T	H	A	N	K
5	29	36	60	74
11	26	42	53	66
2	30		49	72
14	23	31	55	75
9	27	44	50	61

(continued)

(continued)

TEACHER TIPS

- Make sure you laminate the turkey feathers so you may use them again. Otherwise, they may rip when students pull them off the wall.

- Remember that students in wheelchairs should have movement choices, too. Some choices for these students include pushing themselves in their chair, lying on a scooter, or holding on to a hula hoop while an adult pulls them.

- To keep the bingo markers from getting bumped around when students switch turns, you can create a magnetic bingo card and markers. You may also make the card out of felt and use Velcro markers that will stick when placed on the bingo numbers.

- This activity may be adapted for other holidays or seasons throughout the year. Instead of paper turkey feathers with the word "thank" on the bingo card, try Easter eggs and "bunny" at Easter, cupids and "heart" around Valentine's Day, and shamrocks and "lucky" on St. Patrick's Day.

Object Manipulation Activities

2

Snowmen Versus Elves

OBJECTIVE

Students practice throwing skills by trying to knock down the other team's mascots. This is a fun activity to use around Christmas or other seasonal holidays.

EQUIPMENT

- ✫ Bowling pins (at least 10)
- ✫ Paper cutouts of snowmen and elves (at least five of each)
- ✫ Yarn balls and small foam balls
- ✫ Divider cones for the middle line (floor tape or rope would work as well)

SETUP

Divide the playing area in half with cones, floor tape, or rope. Neither team may step past this middle line when throwing. Tape the paper cutouts onto the bowling pins. On the snowmen side of the court, place five snowmen bowling pins toward the back of the playing area. On the elves side of the court, do the same with their five elf bowling pins. You should be the judge of distance and set up accordingly, depending on the skills of your students.

INSTRUCTIONS

1. Divide students equally into two teams. One team is the snowmen, and the other team is the elves.
2. Put teams on their correct side of the playing area, with their mascot cones behind them.
3. To begin play, roll out several yarn balls and small foam balls on each team's side.
4. Students pick up balls on their side, and everyone throws at the same time. The students throw across the middle line, trying to hit the other team's target pins. When students see a ball come across to their side, they may try to block it from hitting their elves or snowmen; they can then throw the ball back across. Once a pin has been knocked over, students may not set it back up.
5. The round finishes when a team has knocked over all the other team's mascots.

TEACHER TIPS

☆ This activity works best if there is a raised surface (e.g., tables, stools, mats) that you can place the bowling pins on behind each team. This enables students to aim at a target that is waist to eye level, instead of throwing straight down to the ground. The raised target creates a more gamelike situation involving skills that students would use in real life (e.g., throwing to a person at a base).

☆ For students who may become confused about where to throw because the constant activity is too much to take in, you can conduct this game in shifts. First, the snowmen team comes onto the court and has two minutes to knock down as many elf pins as they can. Then the team comes off, and the elves team comes on the court for their turn. This can help the students' understanding of what target they are supposed to be throwing at.

☆ For a greater challenge, have varied levels of targets. One pin could be on the ground, one on a chair, one on top of a tall mat standing up, and so forth. This is a great way to check for true aiming versus luck in throwing at a row of pins.

☆ Be creative about other seasonal ideas for the cutouts (e.g., hearts versus cupids, leprechauns versus shamrocks, or scarecrows versus pumpkins).

Rainbow Hoop Shoot

OBJECTIVE

Students practice the skills of dribbling and shooting a basketball while moving around the gym and trying to collect a rainbow of clothespins.

EQUIPMENT

- ✺ Basketball hoops (as many as possible)
- ✺ Basketballs or other balls of the appropriate size and weight
- ✺ Jump ropes
- ✺ Painted clothespins (enough for each student to have one of every color)

SETUP

Place portable basketball hoops in each of the four corners of the gym. If you have small preschool-sized hoops, use these as well. When I set up this game, I use the two regular-sized hoops in the gym (lowered as far as possible), two portable basketball hoops on wheels, a backboard and basket that goes on the top of a door, and a couple preschool-sized hoops.

Paint or color wooden clothespins. If you have eight students in your class and six baskets to shoot at, you'll need six different colors and eight clothespins of each color.

Clip all the same color of clothespins onto one jump rope. Tie or tape a jump rope on a wall near every basket. For example, the tall hoop has a jump rope full of white clothespins hanging near it, the low basket has a jump rope full of purple clothespins hanging near it, and so forth. Every hoop has its own jump rope lined with clothespins of a different color.

INSTRUCTIONS

1. Give each student her own ball. Students will be working individually toward the objective.
2. On your "go" signal, students dribble the ball to the basket of their choice and take a shot.
3. If the students make the basket, they unclip a clothespin from that hoop's jump rope and clip it onto their shirt or pants. Then they choose another basket and dribble there.
4. If they miss the shot, students try again at the same basket. I set a limit of three attempts at one basket; after three attempts, a student must choose another basket to dribble to. Otherwise, some students may spend the entire time trying to score a basket at the highest hoop

without having any success—and without getting any clothespins, for that matter.

5. The activity ends when students have clipped a clothespin on their shirt from each basket, thus collecting a rainbow of clothespins.

TEACHER TIPS

⭐ If some students finish much earlier than the rest of the class, encourage them to try the game in reverse. Once they make a basket, they remove the matching clothespin from their shirt or pants and clip it back onto that basket's jump rope.

⭐ For students who use wheelchairs or walkers, provide a variety of baskets and targets at an appropriate height. Garbage cans, net floor targets, and preschool hoops are all good options to help these students have more success.

Pop That Bubble!

OBJECTIVE

Students try to catch and pop bubbles while seated on a scooterboard.

EQUIPMENT

- Bubbles and blowing wands
- Foam paddles
- Scooters
- Electric bubble machine (if available)

SETUP

Prepare your bubbles and wands, or your bubble machine. In a perfect world, every physical education teacher would have an electric bubble machine. I invested 10 dollars in a bubble machine this year because of this popular game. Before I got the machine, I would become winded during the game, and I couldn't keep up with the chants of "More, more, more bubbles!" This is a great filler activity for those last five minutes of class when you need an extra activity that does not take a lot of time.

INSTRUCTIONS

1. Each student sits on a scooter and holds a foam paddle in his hand. All students participate in this activity at the same time.
2. Begin blowing bubbles, or turn on the bubble machine. Instruct students to go pop those bubbles!
3. Students must stay seated on their scooters the entire time. With paddles in the air, students maneuver around and try to pop as many bubbles as they can. Make sure you keep blowing the bubbles in different directions (whether using wands or a machine) so that students are forced to move around instead of just sitting on their scooters in the same place. Also, you should direct the bubbles upward as you're blowing. This will help ensure that students have time to scooter over and get underneath the bubbles. If you have extra wands and bottles, you can ask for a helper to blow bubbles with you.
4. The activity ends when all students have had a turn to pop bubbles, or when you run out of bubble solution.

TEACHER TIPS

✪ Use this as a jumping activity. Instead of sitting on scooters, students run around and jump up to pop bubbles. They try to pop the highest bubble they can by jumping.

✪ Instead of a paddle, an oversized foam mitten works great for students who are unable to grip a handle or other object. The fitted foam mitten still acts and feels like an extension, and students often find that it is more fun than just popping bubbles with their own fingers.

✪ Challenge students to hold or wear the paddle with their nondominant hand and still pop as many bubbles as possible.

Pick a Piece of Pumpkin

OBJECTIVE

Students dribble a ball and collect felt pieces to complete their team's pumpkin face.

EQUIPMENT

- ✪ Rubber playground balls
- ✪ Cones
- ✪ Orange and green felt (for pumpkins and face pieces)
- ✪ Tape

SETUP

Cut two large pumpkin shapes out of orange felt (one for each team). With a black marker, draw the outline of eyes, nose, mouth, ears, eyebrows, stem, and so forth on each pumpkin. Hang one team's empty pumpkin face on one end wall, and hang the other team's pumpkin on the opposite wall. Place a starting cone for each team near their pumpkin. For each team, cut out pieces of green felt to fit the outlined face parts on their pumpkin. Tape each individual face part on different walls around the gym and at various heights.

INSTRUCTIONS

1. Divide students into two teams and place each team at their starting cone near their empty pumpkin face.
2. Give each team one rubber playground ball for dribbling.
3. The first person on each team begins dribbling the ball under control and moving around the gym. The players choose a face part, dribble over to it, and take it off the wall.
4. Players then dribble back to their team's pumpkin, stick the felt piece on the matching outline, and hand the ball off to the second team member.
5. The next teammate dribbles to another place in the gym that has a different face part, pulls that face part off the wall, dribbles back to stick it on the team's pumpkin face, and so on.
6. The activity ends when both teams have collected all felt pieces and have a complete pumpkin face.

TEACHER TIPS

✩ If possible, use two different colors of felt for the face pieces. This will help students identify which pieces belong to each team. For example, team 1 collects the green face pieces on the wall, and team 2 collects the black pieces.

✩ Use this activity to help students work on different types of skills. Instead of dribbling a ball with their hands, students could collect face pieces by

  ✩ dribbling a ball with their feet,

  ✩ dribbling a ball or puck with a hockey stick,

  ✩ tossing and catching a beanbag in the air while moving, or

  ✩ striking a balloon in the air while moving.

Comic Book Clash

OBJECTIVE

While seated on a scooter, students kick a large exercise ball toward the opposing team's targets of comic book superhero or villain characters.

EQUIPMENT

- ✪ Pictures of superhero and villain characters
- ✪ Cones
- ✪ Large fitness exercise ball
- ✪ Dowel rods or hockey sticks
- ✪ Scooters
- ✪ Floor tape

SETUP

There's always a comic book fan to be found among students! I made up this game during one-on-one time with a student who knew his comic book characters. I found that if I could get creative in my presentation, this student was willing to practice skills he otherwise was not willing to do. In this game, one team represents villain characters, and the other team represents super-hero characters. To set up, get pictures of the characters. (You might want to let your students suggest characters.)

Cut out and tape each picture to the end of a dowel rod. Mark a middle line in the playing area with floor tape; each team's scooters must not cross over this line. Place four to eight cones behind the playing area on each side. Then insert the dowel rods in the holes at the top of the cones so that the characters can be seen from far away.

INSTRUCTIONS

1. Divide students into two teams and place them on their own side of the playing area.
2. Each student sits on a scooter. Students must stay seated on their scooter while kicking, and they may only use their feet for this game.
3. Roll out a large exercise ball onto the playing area. When the ball comes to their side of the playing area, students kick it across toward the other team's targets. If the ball rolls to them, students may block it with their feet or knees, but they may not use their hands.
4. Students continue kicking back and forth, knocking targets over. Once a target has been knocked over, it may not be set back up.

5. The activity ends when all targets on either the villain side or the superhero side have been knocked over.

TEACHER TIPS

✕ If you do not have dowel rods, you may also attach the character pictures to the blades of hockey sticks. In this case, you push the shaft of the stick through a cone to hold it in place.

✕ Once students understand the concept of the game, add one or two additional exercise balls so there's more action.

✕ Instead of having students kick exercise balls, turn this game into scooter hockey, using miniature hockey sticks and yarn balls to shoot at the targets. When playing this way, tape your pictures of characters onto bowling pins (which are knocked over easier with yarn balls).

Bolster Bowling

OBJECTIVE

After completing strength exercises, students use an exercise ball to knock down upright bolster rolls.

EQUIPMENT

- ✬ Cylinder bolsters (rolls). You might find these in physical therapy catalogs.
- ✬ Large exercise balls
- ✬ Gymnastics mat or padded surface

SETUP

Place two or three cylindrical bolsters together on a mat or other padded surface.

INSTRUCTIONS

One upper- and lower-body activity that I use in class involves having students lie prone (facedown) on a large exercise ball. I roll them forward to touch the floor with their hands, and I support their body weight as they push against the floor and roll themselves back to their feet. However, I've noticed that with my support, some students make me do more work than necessary. While I am rolling them back and forth, expecting students to support their own weight, my "support" often causes the exercise to become just a ride. To get the desired outcome, I came up with this activity. Cylindrical bolsters are often quite heavy and weighted, but they work great for lying on and rolling. When you place two or three together, it is fun for students to lie on their bellies or back and push off a wall with either their hands or feet (rolling the cylinders as they move). I set the following short progression to motivate students for their strength exercises:

1. Students do 10 rolls back and forth from hands to feet on an exercise ball. Once they have completed that task, they earn that exercise ball to use for bowling. If you have another exercise ball, you can have the students complete another 10 rolls to earn that second bowling ball.

2. Leave the exercise balls where they are and move to the cylinder bolsters. The student lies on their belly on top of the bolsters. The student's head should be positioned near a wall so that the student pushes off the wall with her arms (completing 10 hard pushes). It works well if you are kneeling behind the student (where she is rolling toward). You may simply push the student's flexed legs forward to roll her on the cylinders back to the wall for her next push.

3. Once this exercise is completed, students stand the cylinder bolsters up on end (we pretend they are trees) and use the exercise balls they earned to bowl the trees over. Because the bolsters are often quite heavy, it takes a hefty roll to knock them down. Place a poly spot or other floor marker at an appropriate distance for individual students to stand on when they bowl down the trees.

4. The activity ends when students have completed the strength training exercises and bowled down the bolsters.

TEACHER TIPS

⭐ I have found that a wheelchair ramp works well for students who are not able to produce enough force to knock down the cylinder bolsters. Position the ramp close to the tree so that the tree wobbles and falls over when students push the exercise ball down the ramp.

⭐ Repeat step 2 of the exercises. This time, have students lie either supine (faceup) or prone (facedown) on the bolsters and push off the wall using their legs. Spot them from behind (near their head) or by their side so they don't roll off the set of bolsters.

Trim That Tree!

OBJECTIVE

Students work together as a team to trim the undecorated Christmas tree by collecting tree decorations and taping them to the tree.

EQUIPMENT

- One large undecorated Christmas tree (cut out of paper)
- Laminated cutouts of various tree decorations
- Scotch tape
- Equipment specific to the skill you want students to practice (e.g., a paddle and balloon, a ball to dribble, or a soccer ball to kick)

SETUP

Cut a very large Christmas tree out of green paper. I make mine about 5 feet (1.5 meters) tall so that lots of decorations will fit on it and so students will have many turns during the activity. Tape the large undecorated paper tree to a wall, at a height that everyone is able to reach. Cut out a variety of objects for the Christmas tree decorations (stocking, candy cane, bell, star, and so forth). Make enough so there are four or five for each student. Tape these decorations on the wall next to the undecorated tree.

INSTRUCTIONS

This activity is the same concept as Pick a Piece of Pumpkin, except all students try to decorate one tree together instead of in separate teams.

1. Students start together in a group next to the undecorated tree.
2. One or two students perform the specified motor skill (see "Teacher Tips" for ideas) down to the end line and back.
3. On returning, students choose a decoration from the wall and tape it to the tree.
4. The activity ends when all decorations have been taken off the wall and you have a trimmed Christmas tree.

TEACHER TIPS

- To quickly create the tree decorations, print off colored pictures from a holiday Web site that contains clip art.
- Here are some ideas for skills that students can practice while collecting the tree decorations:

- Dribble a soccer ball to the opposite wall and back.
- Paddle a balloon in the air to the opposite wall and back.
- Complete an obstacle course. Each time a student gets to the end line, the student gets to choose one decoration and tape it on the tree.
- Dribble a playground ball with one hand (switch hands on the way back to the tree).
- Bounce on a Hoppity Hop ball to the opposite wall and back.
- Dribble a puck with a hockey stick.

Basketball ABCs

OBJECTIVE

Students try to collect all 26 letters of the alphabet by making baskets in various levels of hoops.

EQUIPMENT

- ✬ Basketball hoops
- ✬ Basketballs (of the appropriate weight and size for your students)
- ✬ Alphabet letter cards

SETUP

Write one letter of the alphabet on each of 26 individual recipe cards. Tape all the cards on the wall near the basketball hoops. These cards should be all mixed up, taped in random order and heights on the wall. Across the gym on a separate wall, place the letter *A* where you'd like the alphabet order to start.

This activity works best and allows the most practice when you have three basketball hoops set at various heights. I use a regular basketball hoop lowered to 8 feet (2.4 meters), a portable hoop that's set at about 6 feet (1.8 meters), and a plastic preschool-sized hoop that is low enough for all students to reach.

INSTRUCTIONS

1. Place the students in a line in front of the highest basketball hoop.
2. The first student in line is given the basketball. This student takes one shot at the highest hoop.
3. If the student makes the shot, his turn is over, and he passes the ball to the next person in line. After passing the ball, the student runs over to the wall, finds the letter *B*, and places it next to the *A* on the opposite wall.
4. If students miss their first shot, they get the rebound, move to the medium-sized basket, and take a shot. If they miss again, they move to the lowest hoop. As soon as a basket is made, that student's turn is over, and the student passes the ball to the next person in line before retrieving the next letter of the alphabet.
5. The activity ends when all 26 letters of the alphabet are taped in order on the wall.

TEACHER TIPS

☆ For students who use wheelchairs or walkers, be creative about setting up the three different levels of targets (e.g., garbage cans, net beanbag catchers, adapted basketball hoops). Make sure that every student will have a 100 percent success rate on the third basket so that everyone will always get to choose a letter card after their turn.

☆ Laminate your alphabet cards and use masking tape rolls on the back. This will help ensure that students won't break off the tape when transferring the card from wall to wall.

☆ If the group is able to follow directions at a higher cognitive level, have two students shoot at once so that students get more activity time.

Balance and Coordination Activities

Fish for Your Name

OBJECTIVE

Students practice balancing as they move across a beam while trying to catch fish with a magnetic fishing pole.

EQUIPMENT

- ✦ Balance beams (one or two)
- ✦ Fishing pole with a magnetic "hook"
- ✦ Magnetic fish cutouts
- ✦ Tape

SETUP

- ✦ **Fish:** Print or draw a variety of colorful tropical fish approximately 8 inches (20 centimeters) in length. You will need enough fish for all the letters in your students' first names. Print one letter of the alphabet boldly on the front of each fish. Next, cut out a flat piece of magnetic stripping and glue it on the front of the fish. Place all the fish (letter side up) on the floor next to the balance beam, with some on each side of the beam.

- ✦ **Fishing pole:** To make a fishing pole, tie a piece of string to a wooden yardstick. At the end of the string (where the hook would be), tape on a larger magnet. I like to use the flat magnetic end of a "hide-a-key" box (a small box used to hide a key underneath a car or outside a house). This flat box works well to keep the pole weighted and is easy for students to drop down on the fish of their choice.

INSTRUCTIONS

1. Hand a fishing pole to the first student in line. One at a time, students walk forward or sideways across the beam, looking for letters in their name.

2. When students spot a fish with their letter on it, they drop the fishing pole's hook (i.e., magnet) on top of that fish. Once they catch a fish with the first letter in their name, they walk the remainder of the beam, and then go tape that fish letter on a designated spot on the wall.

3. After hanging the first fish on the wall, that same student begins again on the balance beam, fishes for the next letter in her name, and so on.

4. A student's turn ends when she has spelled out her first name on the wall using the fish letters she has caught.

TEACHER TIPS

- ✦ Make sure you have determined the duplicate letters you'll need to make in order for your students to spell out their names. Chances are, you'll need to make multiple fish with frequently used letters such as *E, R,* or *A*.

 Students in a wheelchair may fish right from their chair, and then wheel themselves over to the wall to tape up their fish letters.

 Use this as one of many activity stations to avoid having students waiting in line while another student is fishing for letters. If you want to have two students fishing at the same time, push two balance beams together.

 You can buy 8-by-10-inch magnetic sheets that may be cut to the actual shape of the fish. Then just glue your colored fish pictures to the magnetic paper. That way, there are no small magnet tabs that might fall off.

 Another option would be to use Velcro to catch the fish.

 Laminate your fish before using them so they last longer.

Watch Your Step

OBJECTIVE

Students practice balancing as they walk across a beam while transferring Kush balls from the beam to the top of cones.

EQUIPMENT

- Two balance beams
- Kush balls
- Tall construction cones

SETUP

Push two balance beams together end to end so they form one long beam. Place a Kush ball on top of the beam every three or four steps; there should be approximately five to seven balls to pick up during each turn.

Set a large construction cone to the side of the balance beam next to each Kush ball (alternating sides). Students will try to place the Kush ball on the top hole of each cone so that it stays on the cone. You need to get this large cone positioned just right because it will add to the students' practice in body positioning and balance. The cone should be just out of arm's reach for the students, forcing them to lift one foot slightly from the beam.

INSTRUCTIONS

1. Students line up at one end of the balance beam.
2. Students take turns walking in a heel-to-toe pattern across the balance beam. When they come to the first Kush ball, they carefully bend down and pick it up while maintaining their balance on the beam. They balance and stretch to distribute the Kush ball to the top of the cone on the right side of the balance beam. A few steps later, they will come to the next Kush ball, distribute it to the top of the cone on the left side of the beam, and so on.
3. A student's turn ends when all Kush balls have been picked up and placed on the cones.
4. The student should place the Kush balls back on the beam to help reset for the next person's turn.

TEACHER TIPS

- To help decrease the reset time between turns, stick a small piece of bright floor tape on the balance beam at each spot where a Kush ball is to be set. Then students will know right where to place the balls when resetting for the next student.

⚝ For another challenge, try putting the two balance beams side to side with a 2-foot (61-centimeter) gap in the middle. Have students try the same activity while moving in a straddle position.

⚝ To minimize wait time, use this as one of several stations. A maximum of three or four students should be at the activity at one time.

⚝ Another idea to increase activity time would be to use one extra long beam, consisting of three or more balance beams pushed together. In this case, the next student may mount the balance beam once the student in front of him has reached the second beam. Have extra Kush balls ready to reset as students pick up balls so the activity moves continuously.

⚝ To increase the duration of a student's turn, have students walk both directions on the balance beam. Once a student has placed the Kush balls on the cones, she can turn around and walk the opposite direction on the balance beam, back to the starting line. When walking back, she reaches for the Kush balls on the cones and sets them back on the balance beam.

Balance Beam Basketball

OBJECTIVE
Students balance across the beams while picking up balls and shooting them in targets as they walk.

EQUIPMENT
- ✬ Balance beams (at least two pushed together)
- ✬ O-rings (foam deck rings)
- ✬ Basketballs or other balls of the appropriate weight
- ✬ Basketball hoops, targets, or buckets to shoot in

SETUP
Push two or three long balance beams together lengthwise, making an extra long beam. Every five steps, place an O-ring on the balance beam. This acts as a ball holder. Place a ball in each O-ring for students to pick up as they are walking across the beam. Position targets for students to shoot at perpendicular to each O-ring marker. Place the targets so they alternate—with the first target to the right of the beam, the second on the left, and so on.

INSTRUCTIONS
1. Students take turns walking across the beam. When they come to an O-ring, they pick up that ball and shoot it at the target perpendicular to them.
2. Students then step over the O-ring and continue balancing until they reach the next ball.
3. After walking the length of the beams and shooting all balls at the targets, the student helps retrieve the balls and set them back on the O-rings for the next person's turn.
4. The activity ends after each student has had a set number of turns to balance and shoot.

TEACHER TIPS
- ✬ To increase the challenge, use various sizes and textures of balls.
- ✬ Vary the level of targets based on the abilities of your students. Set up the balance beam near a regular high hoop to use that as one target.

★ Challenge students by changing the way they need to move on the balance beam. For example, require students to walk forward the first time across, walk sideways on the beam the second time across, and walk backward the third time across.

★ To keep students active, those waiting in line may be the ball retrievers and set the balls back on the O-rings. This will keep the activity moving more rapidly.

★ This game is designed for a group of no more than five students. If you have a large class, use this as one of many stations to allow maximum activity time.

★ Use floor tape to make a line on the floor parallel to the balance beams. Students who use a walker or wheelchair may wheel along this line and shoot at targets of appropriate height. Have a peer follow the student and hand him a ball to shoot as he comes to each target.

Shake, Balance, and Go!

OBJECTIVE

Students practice the skill of balancing various objects on different body parts while moving.

EQUIPMENT

- ✫ One large foam die
- ✫ Body part picture cards
- ✫ Various items to balance (e.g., juggling scarves, beanbags, small stuffed animals, Hacky Sacks, and so on)
- ✫ Dome cones
- ✫ One hula hoop
- ✫ Bucket or garbage can

SETUP

Draw or print pictures of the following six body parts: head, shoulder, foot, elbow, knee, and belly. These pictures should be approximately the size of a recipe card. Cut out the body part pictures and tape them over the numbered dots of a large foam die.

At one end line of the gym, spread out many dome cones in random placements 2 feet (61 centimeters) away from each other. I set out enough for 5 to 10 cones per student. Under each cone, hide one of the objects to balance (juggling scarf, beanbag, Hacky Sack, and so forth). There should be a variety of objects, but only one under each cone. These should be smaller objects with a material that is soft enough to conform to the body and allow students success in balancing and moving. Items that have beans or sand inside them—such as beanbags or Hacky Sacks—work well. Place the hula hoop and foam die at the opposite end line of the gym, along with a large bucket or garbage can.

INSTRUCTIONS

1. Tell students to start by the hula hoop on the end line.
2. Choose one student to be the first die shaker. This student rolls the die inside the hula hoop for everyone to see. When the die has stopped moving, ask students what it landed on (e.g., head, elbow, and so forth). This roll determines what body part students will use to balance the object they are about to retrieve.
3. All the students run down to the cone area and choose one cone to look under. They take the object that is under that cone and replace the cone right side up. If there is no object under the first cone they

check, they look under others until they find an object to balance. Each student places her item on her elbow, head, or whatever was rolled and then moves carefully back to the hula hoop starting marker, balancing the object as she goes. Depending on the shake of the die, students will need to move slowly on their feet, hopping at times, or even crab walking if the belly side of the die was rolled.

4. Once all students return to the hula hoop, they drop their objects in the bucket, and a different shaker is chosen. The new student shakes the die, announces the body part, and so on.

5. The activity ends when all objects under the cones are gone and every student has had at least one turn to be a shaker.

TEACHER TIPS

✩ To add a greater challenge, hide a couple of hard, nonconforming objects such as a tennis ball or wooden block under certain cones. These will prove to be more of a challenge to balance. Don't hide too many, however, or students might get frustrated.

✩ Students in wheelchairs may still balance objects on all body parts. For students who use a walker, you should assist them, if needed, in getting the object placed on their heads or shoulders so that their arms are still supporting them in their walkers.

✩ If students using walkers or wheelchairs are able to use their arms, another option is to give them a plastic Frisbee to hold while they are moving. They use this Frisbee as the body part and try to balance the object and keep it inside the Frisbee as they wheel or walk back.

Don't Drop Your Ice Cream

OBJECTIVE

Students try to fill up an empty ball pit with balls while practicing locomotor skills, balance, and eye–hand coordination.

EQUIPMENT

- Cardboard paper towel tubes
- Kiddie swimming pool or ball pit container
- Lots of small balls (plastic, yarn, foam, and so forth)
- Cones

SETUP

Place a starting cone for each team at the half-court line, and place an empty kiddie pool at the end line near the wall. All the balls are placed on the floor against the opposite end wall from the swimming pool.

INSTRUCTIONS

1. Divide students into teams of two people. To begin, teams stand behind their starting cone.
2. Give one empty paper towel tube to each team.
3. The first person on each team runs to the pile of balls ("ice cream factory"), chooses one ball ("scoop of ice cream"), and runs back to the team's starting cone.
4. Once back at the starting cone, students place the ice cream on the paper towel tube (ice cream cone) that the other teammate is holding.
5. That second student balances the ball on the tube while moving down to the empty pool, drops the ball in the pool, runs back, and hands off the tube to his teammate.
6. Students then switch roles of moving and balancing. If an ice cream scoop falls off of a student's cone in route to the swimming pool, you can have the student either begin again from the team's starting cone or just replace the ball and continue on (depending on skill level). You may always adjust the distance that students must travel while balancing the ball, according to the success level students are achieving.
7. The activity ends when all the balls are carried to the pool.

TEACHER TIPS

☆ Now that you have a swimming pool full of balls, what do you do with it? You may let students take turns jumping in the ice cream dish, or you could have students play Case of the Missing Spiders (see page 72 in chapter 4).

☆ For a greater challenge, call out a locomotor movement (e.g., run, hop, skip, gallop, slide) that students must do as they move to get a ball.

☆ For higher-skilled students, you may even vary how they must move with their paper towel tube while balancing the ball (i.e., backward, sideways, on their knees, and so on). Remind them that slow and steady is the best strategy for that part of the activity.

☆ If students are frustrated or unable to balance the ball with the paper towel tube, you can use a larger foam ball and have students balance it inside a Frisbee or the center of an O-ring.

☆ To increase the challenge, use colored floor tape to make a line leading from each team's cone to the kiddie pool. Tell students they must balance on this line while walking with their tube and ball. Very tricky!

Dot-to-Dot

OBJECTIVE

Students practice coordination and balance by performing various challenges on colored poly spots.

EQUIPMENT

- ✵ Floor tape
- ✵ Colored poly spots
- ✵ Board game spinner with four colors that match the poly spots
- ✵ Padded floor mats (optional)

SETUP

Choose four colors of poly spots and line them up in rows along the floor of the gym, in a grid of four spots by six spots. Each should be evenly spaced from the next, approximately one foot (about a third of a meter) from each other. All the same colored dots should line up, so there is a row of six blue spots, six yellow spots, and so on.

Write out a list of the various balance and coordination tasks you would like your students to practice. These can be written on a note card; you will be holding this card and calling out the various challenges. I usually use this activity as a warm-up or as one of several stations around the gym. Two or three students participate on each grid of 24 poly spots. The following are some ideas for the challenges to call out. The blank lines indicate where you will spin the board game spinner and call out a color.

- ✵ Ski jump side to side 10 times between *blue* and *yellow.*
- ✵ Hop on one foot from _____ to _____ 8 times.
- ✵ Balance for 10 seconds, with one hand on _____ and one foot on _____.
- ✵ Bear walk to the end of the mat with your left hand and foot on _____ and your right hand and foot on _____.
- ✵ With one foot on _____ and the other on _____, do a two-foot jump over the dots in front of you, and land on the same colors.
- ✵ With only one foot touching the ground, balance on _____ to the count of 15 bananas.
- ✵ Balance with your head on _____ and one foot on _____.
- ✵ Balance with two feet on the same _____ dot and two hands on the same _____ dot.

INSTRUCTIONS

1. Each student stands on a poly spot, at least two dots away from the next student. Everyone participates at the same time in this activity.

2. Explain to students that you will be spinning the spinner to find out the colors they will need to touch when doing the coordination tasks. Give them an example such as "Balance with one foot on _____." Hold up the spinner and let the students see you spin it. If it lands on red, that is the first fill-in-the-blank color. "Balance with one foot on *red* and one foot on _____." Spin the spinner a second time to fill in this blank. It must be a different color from the first spin. If it lands on red again, spin until it lands on a new color (e.g., blue). Repeat the challenge out loud again: "Balance with one foot on *red* and one foot on *blue*."

3. Continue using this format with your list of written challenges, pausing and spinning the spinner whenever you need a color to fill in a blank.

4. The activity ends when all students have attempted your entire list of balance and coordination tasks.

(continued)

(continued)

TEACHER TIPS

☆ If you don't have a board game spinner, you may color Popsicle sticks and draw them out of a can to randomly select the colors. Or you could tape cards of the matching poly spot colors onto the sides of a large foam die. Roll the die for each challenge, announcing the color that it lands on.

☆ Students who use walkers or wheelchairs may play this game lying on the floor (out of their chair). Place several gymnastics mats together, and tape down the edges of the poly spots on top of the mats. Students may lie on the mat and be given challenges to do with their arms, legs, or other able parts. Here are some sample challenges for these students:

   ☆ Do 5 hand slaps between a _____ and a _____ dot.

   ☆ Army crawl to the end of the mat with one elbow on _____ and the other on _____. (You must spin neighboring colors for this task.)

   ☆ Do 10 heel kicks from a _____ to a _____ dot.

   ☆ Roll from the _____ row to the _____ row and back 3 times.

Combination
Activities

Ball Pit Bulldozer

OBJECTIVE

Students fill up an empty ball pit area in a fun way! They gather balls by scootering around the gym and shoot baskets into a tunnel that later gets "bulldozed" into the ball pit.

EQUIPMENT

- Flexible crawl-through tunnel
- Small balls (e.g., yarn, plastic, foam)
- Empty ball pit (e.g., plastic kiddie swimming pool)
- Exercise ball (a size that will fit through the tunnel opening)
- Scooters

SETUP

Spread out a bunch of small balls on the ground, all around the playing area. Place a tunnel in the middle of the gym. You will be stretching the tunnel up on end, holding the top opening toward the ceiling (you determine the appropriate height) for students to shoot balls into, similar to a basket.

INSTRUCTIONS

1. Each student has a scooter. Students sit on their scooters and move around the playing area, collecting balls.
2. When they get a ball, students take it and scooter over to the tunnel in the middle of the gym.
3. Students try to score a basket by throwing the ball in the top opening so it drops all the way through the tunnel and lands on the floor inside.
4. Once students have collected all the balls and shot them into the tunnel, you should choose one student who would like to be the bulldozer.
5. Carefully lay the tunnel down on the ground so that all the balls that have been dropped in will be at one end. Place the empty swimming pool at the other end of the tunnel.
6. The bulldozer takes the large exercise ball and starts at the end with all the small balls. With everyone's cheers to "Bulldoze!" that student pushes the large exercise ball through the tunnel, which in turn pushes all the small balls into the ball pit.
7. Keep those balls in the swimming pool, but roll out others around the gym for the next round. Once these have been collected and shot in the tunnel, choose a new bulldozer to push them through.

8. Repeat as necessary until everyone has had a turn to bulldoze into the ball pit.

9. Let students enjoy the filled pit by jumping and playing in the balls.

TEACHER TIPS

✫ Students who are not able to crawl through the tunnel may lie on the ground and kick or push the large ball through the tunnel to push the small balls out.

✫ Think of other ways for students to do the ball collecting (instead of using scooters). Here are some ideas:

  ✫ Conduct the activity as a race—students run to collect the balls as fast as they can.

  ✫ Have students use bikes with baskets connected to them to carry the balls.

  ✫ Have students switch locomotor skills (e.g., hop, jump, skip, gallop).

  ✫ Call out various animals, and have students move like those animals while collecting the balls (e.g., kangaroo, eagle, snake, cheetah, frog).

✫ Add some extra strength, balance, and cardiorespiratory exercise by having the bulldozers do 20 seated bounces on the exercise ball before getting to use it to bulldoze through the tunnel.

Ready, Set, Pull!

OBJECTIVE

Students use upper- and lower-body strength to pull a partner across the floor (while the partner is sitting or lying on a blanket).

EQUIPMENT

- Old blankets or bed sheets (large)
- Bowling pins
- Yarn balls
- Cones

SETUP

Place a starting cone or line where the blankets are, and place an end cone where the puller needs to go around with the blanket rider.

INSTRUCTIONS

1. Pair up students, making sure that partners are close in weight and able to pull each other.
2. The first person lies down or sits pretzel style on the blanket, and his partner pulls him around the end cone and back to the starting cone.
3. Once they get back to the starting line, students switch positions.
4. The activity ends when all students have had turns being the puller and the rider, and when partners have completed the specified number of pulls.

TEACHER TIPS

- For a fun challenge, set up a long row of bowling pins from the starting line to the finish line (approximately 15 to 20 pins). Set these pins off the pulling track so there is about 8 feet (2.4 meters) between the pins and where the blanket travels. The riders load up with 10 yarn balls to hold on their blanket. As they are being pulled down the track, they launch the balls (using an overhand or underhand throw) from their seated position on the blanket and try to knock over the pins. Once the partners get to the finish line, you should reset any pins that were knocked over. The partners return to the starting line and switch roles, and a new student gets ready for a ride.

- ✨ Students who are not able to sit up on the blanket by themselves may use a wedge. Place a wedge on top of the blanket or sheet and recline the student safely on the wedge.

- ✨ For a student who is not able to throw a ball, have him use a foam paddle, or place an oversized mitt on his hand. The blanket should be pulled down the line one to two feet (about half a meter) from the line of pins. At this distance, the students can try to reach out (while lying down) and knock over the pins with their paddle.

Rainbow Snow Tower

OBJECTIVE

Students work together to see how large a snow tower they can build. Then they decorate the tower with different colors.

EQUIPMENT

☆ Snow fort brick molds or empty ice cream buckets
☆ Spray bottles
☆ Water
☆ Food coloring
☆ Cone

SETUP

Here's another fun outdoor activity to use during the winter. Make sure you choose a day when the snow is very sticky. Place a cone approximately 15 to 20 feet (4.5 to 6.1 meters) from the area where the snow tower will be built. Collect enough brick molds or empty buckets for each student to have his own. Fill each spray bottle with water and a few drops of food coloring; each bottle should have a different color of water (e.g., red, yellow, green, blue).

INSTRUCTIONS

1. Hand out one bucket or brick mold to each student.
2. Show students the area where the snow tower will be built. Then let the students all work together to pack snow and build a pyramid-shaped tower.
3. When a good-sized tower has been built, tell students to form a line behind the cone.
4. Lay out your spray bottles—each filled with a different color of water—near the tower.
5. The first student in line moves to the snow tower, according to your directions. Some ideas for this movement include crab walk, bear walk, log roll, and run backward.
6. On reaching the snow tower, the student chooses a spray bottle, sprays that color on *one* brick, and returns to the line using the same movement choice.
7. The next person moves down to the tower, chooses another bottle, and sprays a different brick.

8. The activity ends when all the bricks have been sprayed and students have created a beautiful rainbow tower.

TEACHER TIPS

☆ Depending on how attached the students are to their tower, they often enjoy hopping onto sleds and pulling each other through the tower to knock it over.

☆ Let students make snowballs and throw them at the tower to knock it over.

☆ If snow is not available, you may still use this activity. Instead of building a tower out of snow, students take turns collecting bricks or similar-sized boxes or wooden blocks. Cover each brick with an old white tube sock. Cut part of the top elastic off each sock, and simply stretch out and slide the sock over the brick. Hide the white bricks around a playing area. Have students search for them and then build a tower out of all the bricks they find. Once the tower has been built, continue the activity as previously explained, with students spraying the "white" bricks with different colors.

Case of the Missing Spiders

OBJECTIVE

Students move through an obstacle course and then jump in a ball pit to search for rubber spiders.

EQUIPMENT

- ✄ Ball pit (e.g., plastic kiddie swimming pool filled with balls)
- ✄ Rubber spiders (different colors)
- ✄ Equipment for a short obstacle course (e.g., balance beam, scooter, minitrampoline)
- ✄ Starting cone

SETUP

Once you have filled a ball pit or pool with balls, you may use it as a part of this activity. Hide 10 to 20 rubber spiders or bugs (of various solid colors) under the balls in the pool. Set up a few pieces of equipment for a short obstacle course; the ball pit is the last section of the course. For example, set up a starting cone, balance beam, scooter, minitrampoline, and ball pit, in that order.

INSTRUCTIONS

1. Assign each student a color of spider to search for.
2. Line up students behind the starting cone.
3. The first student in line begins at the starting cone, walks across the balance beam, sits on the scooter, and pushes herself over to the minitrampoline. Once the student reaches the minitrampoline, she does 20 bounces. On the last bounce, the student jumps into the ball pit (if needed, use a one- or two-hand assist on this jump). Signal for the next student in line to begin once the person in front of her has reached the scooter.
4. After jumping into the pool (ball pit), the student digs around for a spider until she finds one that is her assigned color.
5. The student brings the spider to you and then goes to the end of the line to get ready for another turn on the obstacle course.
6. The activity ends when all the spiders have been found.

TEACHER TIPS

☆ Digging in a ball pit is great for students who need extra sensory activities. You should fill the pit with balls that include a variety of textures and weights.

☆ A wedge may be used under the balls to help support students who are unable to sit in the pit on their own. Have students search for the spiders, grasp them, and drop them in a bucket near the edge of the ball pit.

Monster Truck Knockdown

OBJECTIVE

Students try to collect stacking cups by completing an obstacle course. As a reward, they take turns driving a remote control truck to knock over the cup tower.

EQUIPMENT

- ✶ Stacking cups
- ✶ Remote control truck or car
- ✶ Obstacle course equipment (hula hoops, Hoppity Hop, tunnel, balance beam, stretch band)
- ✶ Parachute or an extra large blanket or tarp to crawl underneath

SETUP

Set up an obstacle course that involves skills you want your students to work on. An example of a course I use is in the diagram on page 75. Under the parachute section of the obstacle course, hide all the stacking cups.

INSTRUCTIONS

1. Tell students that at the end of the obstacle course, they will crawl under the parachute and come out of the obstacle course with only one cup. Then they will add it to the tower of cups that the whole group is building as a team.

2. Send the first student through the course. (Give a signal for the next student in line to begin the obstacle course once the student in front of her has reached the halfway point through the course.) After getting their cup from under the parachute, students start building the tower. Depending on your class size, once everyone has moved through the course two or three times, there should be enough cups for a good-sized tower.

3. Invite one student to drive the remote control truck into the cups to knock them over.

4. Repeat the activity as time allows, changing truck drivers each time.

TEACHER TIPS

- ✶ If time doesn't allow enough trips through the obstacle course, have everyone just help build the tower up again without going through the course. Keep changing truck drivers so that everyone has a chance to drive and knock over a tower.

☆ Knocking down the tower with the truck is exciting for many students. If a student is overstimulated and chases after the truck as it moves, create a "pit stop" on a poly spot marker where the student needs to stand or sit to drive the truck.

☆ You can use the tower knockdown as a reward in any other activity! It's also a great motivator for fitness stations. For example, after every exercise station they complete, students can grab a cup and bring it over to the tower.

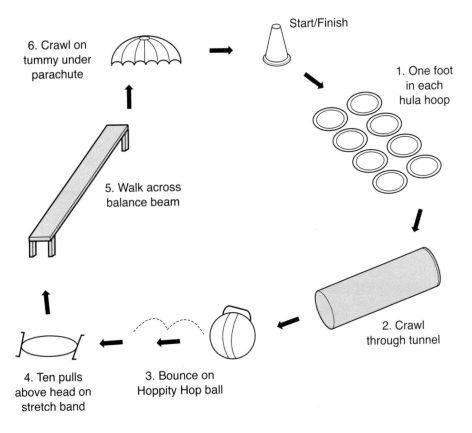

Start/Finish

6. Crawl on tummy under parachute

1. One foot in each hula hoop

5. Walk across balance beam

2. Crawl through tunnel

4. Ten pulls above head on stretch band

3. Bounce on Hoppity Hop ball

(continued)

(continued)

- When thinking of ways that students who use a wheelchair or walker could complete an obstacle course, remember that other students can lend their help and muscles. Instead of hopping on a bouncy ball, a student could lie on a body scooter or large blanket and be pulled by a peer from point A to point B.

- Keep your obstacle course fairly short so that it takes students no longer than two minutes to move through it. This allows for greater activity time for everyone.

- When students crawl under the parachute laid out on the floor, you should have adults (or the students waiting in line) hold the sides of the parachute so it doesn't move around.

Ropes and Towers

OBJECTIVE

Students collect building blocks by completing a strength activity. They use the building blocks to build a tower that they try to knock over.

EQUIPMENT

- ✿ Wooden building blocks (10 per student)
- ✿ Scooters (one regular and one full-body length)
- ✿ Bucket for each student
- ✿ Long ropes (two)
- ✿ S hooks (optional)
- ✿ Yarn balls

SETUP

This game has two parts. The first part is a strength activity in which students collect their blocks. The second part of the game involves building a tower with the blocks and practicing the skill of throwing to knock the tower over.

To set up, dump out a pile of wooden building blocks in the middle of the gym. A good number is 10 blocks per student, which allows a tall tower to be built. Get two long ropes and two scooters. Attach an S hook to the end of each long rope. (For easier grasp, use rope that is thinner than a tug-of-war rope). One rope should be hooked or tied to something on the ground so the rope is lying flat on the floor. The second rope should be tied or hooked to two standards or immovable objects so that it is suspended 2 to 3 feet (about 0.5 to 1 meter) off the ground.

INSTRUCTIONS

1. Give each student a bucket to keep his blocks in.
2. Divide students into two groups, with one group at the end of each rope.
3. Students using the rope on the ground sit or lie on a scooter and pull themselves to the other end using a hand-over-hand pulling motion to propel themselves. If they choose to sit on the scooter, the rope should go under the armpit as they perform a hand-over-hand pull on the rope to move (see the first photo on page 78). If they choose to lie on their belly, the scooter should straddle the rope to allow the scooter to stay on track and not veer off to the side (see the second photo on page 78).

(continued)

(continued)

4. After pulling themselves to the end of the rope, students get to pick a block from the pile and drop it in their bucket.

5. Students then switch lines and go to the second suspended rope.

6. For this rope, students lie on their backs on long, full-body scooters. They pull their weight by reaching above and grasping the rope hand over hand to move backward (headfirst) to the other end (see the third photo on this page).

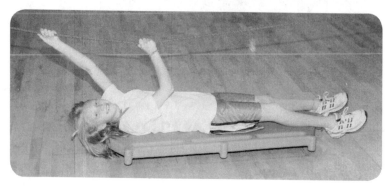

7. After pulling themselves to the end of the rope, students collect another block from the pile and drop it in their bucket.

8. Students continue to switch lines, pull themselves, and collect blocks until they have each collected 10 blocks in their bucket.

9. Tell students to take their bucket and find their own space in the gym.

10. Using all their blocks, they should build a tall tower.

11. Hand out three yarn balls to each student. Position the students at an appropriate distance from their tower, far enough away that they are throwing hard in an overhand motion. They throw their yarn balls and try to knock over their tower.

12. The activity ends when all students have successfully knocked over their tower.

TEACHER TIPS

☆ Instead of having students throw balls to knock down the tower, choose a different object-control skill for the day. Some other ideas are shooting a hockey puck at the tower or kicking a soccer ball to knock it over.

☆ Have students complete an obstacle course to collect their blocks. Each time they get to the finish line, they put one block in their buckets.

☆ Set up various fitness stations, with piles of blocks at each station. When students finish a station's task (e.g., 20 leg raises with a stretch band, 15 jumps on the minitrampoline), they get to take a block from that station and put it in their bucket.

☆ Students who are unable to throw, kick, or strike a ball may use a wheelchair ramp and push a large ball down the ramp to knock over the tower.

About the Author

Kiwi Bielenberg, MEd, has taught elementary physical education since 1996. She received a bachelor's degree in physical education from St. Olaf College and a master's degree in applied kinesiology and adapted physical education from the University of Minnesota in 2002, where her work toward her degree broadened her view of how to creatively adapt games and activities to meet the needs of all students. She is a member of the Minnesota Alliance of Health, Physical Education, Recreation and Dance. In her leisure time she enjoys playing soccer, fishing, playing piano and trumpet, and watching her kids play hockey.